BTEC

Level 2

Tower Hamlets College
Learning Centre
131033

HEALTH AND SOCIAL CARE
ASSESSMENT GUIDE

THE LIBRARY
TOWER HAMLETS COLLEGE
POPLAR HIGH STREET
LONDON E14 0AF
Tel: 0207 510 7763

Unit 3 EFFECTIVE COMMUNICATION IN HEALTH AND SOCIAL CARE

ELIZABETH RASHEED

HODDER
EDUCATION
AN HACHETTE UK COMPANY

The sample learner answers provided in this assessment guide are intended to give guidance on how a learner might approach generating evidence for each assessment criterion. Answers do not necessarily include all of the evidence required to meet each assessment criterion. Assessor comments intend to highlight how sample answers might be improved to help learners meet the requirements of the grading criterion but are provided as a guide only. Sample answers and assessor guidance have not been verified by Edexcel and any information provided in this guide should not replace your own internal verification process.

Any work submitted as evidence for assessment for this unit must be the learner's own. Submitting as evidence, in whole or in part, any material taken from this guide will be regarded as plagiarism. Hodder Education accepts no responsibility for learners plagiarising work from this guide that does or does not meet the assessment criteria.

The sample assignment briefs are provided as a guide to how you might assess the evidence required for all or part of the internal assessment of this unit. They have not been verified or endorsed by Edexcel and should be internally verified through your own lead internal verifier as with any other assignment briefs, and/or checked through the BTEC assignment checking service.

Orders: please contact Bookpoint Ltd, 130 Milton Park, Abingdon, Oxon OX14 4SB. Telephone: +44 (0)1235 827720. Fax: +44 (0)1235 400454. Lines are open from 9.00a.m. to 5.00p.m., Monday to Saturday, with a 24-hour message answering service. You can also order through our website www.hoddereducation.co.uk

If you have any comments to make about this, or any of our other titles, please send them to educationenquiries@hodder.co.uk

British Library Cataloguing in Publication Data

A catalogue record for this title is available from the British Library

ISBN: 978 1444 18971 1

Published 2013

Impression number   10 9 8 7 6 5 4 3 2 1

Year   2016 2015 2014 2013

Copyright © 2013 Elizabeth Rasheed

All rights reserved. No part of this publication may be reproduced or transmitted in any form or by any means, electronic or mechanical, including photocopy, recording, or any information storage and retrieval system, without permission in writing from the publisher or under licence from the Copyright Licensing Agency Limited. Further details of such licences (for reprographic reproduction) may be obtained from the Copyright Licensing Agency Limited, Saffron House, 6–10 Kirby Street, London EC1N 8TS.

Cover photo © Alex Kalmbach – Fotolia.com

Typeset by Integra Software Services Pvt. Ltd., Pondicherry, India

Printed in Dubai for Hodder Education,
an Hachette UK Company,
338 Euston Road,
London NW1 3BH

Contents

Class: 362.1 HET

Accession No: 131033

Type: REF

For the attention of the learner

You are not allowed to copy any information from this book and use it as your own evidence. That would count as plagiarism, which is taken very seriously and may result in disqualification. If you are in any doubt at all please speak to your teacher.

Command words

You will find the following command words in the assessment criteria for each unit.

Analyse	Identify the factors that apply and state how these are related. Explain the importance of each one.
Assess	Give careful consideration to all the factors or events that apply and identify which are the most important or relevant.
Demonstrate	Provide several relevant examples or related evidence which clearly support the arguments you are making. This may include showing practical skills.
Describe	Give a clear description that includes all the relevant features – think of it as 'painting a picture with words'.
Discuss	Consider different aspects of a topic and how they interrelate, and the extent to which they are important.
Evaluate	Bring together all the information and review it to form a conclusion. Give evidence for each of your views or statements.
Explain	Provide details and give reasons and/or evidence to support the arguments being made. Start by introducing the topic then give the 'how' or 'why'.
Summarise	Demonstrate an understanding of the key facts, and if possible illustrate with relevant examples.

Acknowledgments

Photo credits

The authors and publishers would like to thank the following for permission to reproduce material in this book:

p. 6 (top) © Roman Milert - Fotolia.com; p. 7 (bottom) © John Birdsall / Photofusion Pictures; p. 21 © Sandor Kacso – Fotolia.com.

Every effort has been made to trace and acknowledge ownership of copyright. The publishers will be happy to make suitable arrangements with any copyright holders whom it has not been possible to contact.

UNIT 3
Effective Communication in Health and Social Care

Unit 3 Effective Communication in Health and Social Care is an internally assessed, optional, specialist unit with three learning aims:

- Learning aim A: Investigate different forms of communication
- Learning aim B: Investigate barriers to communication in health and social care
- Learning aim C: Communicate effectively in health and social care.

The unit focuses on communication. Clear communication is essential in health and social care in one-to-one situations and also in group situations. In emergencies it can save lives. In less urgent situations it helps people understand their care and helps teams of care workers to give better care.

Learning aim A examines the communication cycle and different types of communication such as speech and body language. It also investigates alternative forms of communication such as British Sign Language (BSL).

Learning aim B investigates a variety of barriers to communication and their effects. It also investigates how to overcome the barriers and the beneficial effects of doing so.

Learning aim C looks at how we communicate effectively with groups and with individuals.

Each learning aim is divided into two sections. The first section focuses on the content of the learning aim and each of the topics is covered. At the end of each section there are some knowledge recap questions to test your understanding of the subject. The answers for the knowledge recap questions can be found at the end of the guide.

The second section of each learning aim provides support with assessment by using evidence generated by a learner, for each grading criterion, with feedback from an assessor. The assessor has highlighted where the evidence is sufficient to satisfy the grading criterion and provided developmental feedback when additional work is required.

At the end of the guide are examples of assignment briefs for this unit. There is a sample assignment for each learning aim, and the tasks allow you to generate the evidence needed to meet all the assessment criteria in the unit.

Learning aim A
Investigate different forms of communication

Assessment criteria

2A.P1 Describe different forms of verbal and non-verbal communication.

2A.P2 Describe different forms of alternative communication for different needs, using examples from health and social care.

2A.M1 Explain the advantages and disadvantages of different forms of communication used, with reference to a one-to-one and a group interaction.

2A.D1 Assess the effectiveness of different forms of communication for service users with different needs.

Topic A.1 Effective communication

Communication is a two-way process. These key elements form the communication cycle:

- **Sender** – the person starting the communication
- **Message** – what the sender wishes to communicate
- **Medium** – the method of communication, whether verbal, written, signed, electronic or telephone
- **Receiver** – the person who receives the message and interprets it
- **Understanding** – the message has to be correctly interpreted by the receiver
- **Feedback** – the receiver needs to show the sender that he or she has received and understood the message.

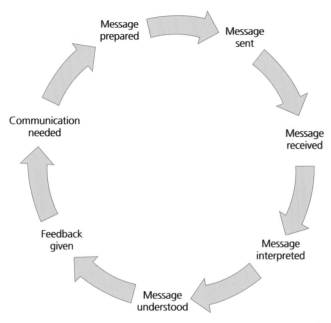

Figure 1.1 The communication cycle

Verbal communication

Verbal communication involves:

- Clear speech. Mumbling or speaking softly will disrupt communication with someone who is partly deaf.
- Using age-appropriate language. Using complicated words with a five-year-old will not help communication.
- Non-discriminatory. When asking a person's name, ask for their first name, not their Christian name. Many people are not Christian and so will not have a Christian name.
- Using appropriate pace, tone and pitch.
- Pace, or the speed at which we communicate, affects whether a message is received and understood. This is especially so if people are hearing a message in a different language to their own. If you are learning French, you may be able to understand if the speaker talks slowly, but not if they speak quickly.
- The tone we use can be aggressive, neutral or friendly.
- The pitch, whether high or low, tells the listener whether the speaker is stressed or relaxed. A high-pitched scream says 'Something is wrong – help'.
- Pitch and tone affect communication. 'Come here' can be a warm invitation or an order, depending on the tone and pitch.
- Active listening skills. The listener may ask a question, nod in agreement or murmur approval. This shows they are receiving and interpreting the message.

Non-verbal communication

Our bodies communicate messages. With effective communication, non-verbal body language supports the message the words are conveying. Sometimes body language shows a different message from what we are saying, confusing the receiver. Examples of non-verbal communication include:

- Posture (how we stand). This should be positive and not defensive, for example, not folding arms.
- Facial expressions should match the message. Use a sympathetic expression when giving bad news. Smiling is not appropriate when doing so.

Figure 1.2 Facial expression should match the message

- Eye contact should be positive – making brief eye contact, not staring aggressively, can be effective communication.
- Appropriate use of touch and personal space. Never assume that people like to be touched. Respond to the individual's needs, not your own. You may want to hug a distressed person but they may not want it. Consider their personal space. If they move away, you are too close.
- Gestures support communication but can also offend people. The 'OK' sign (when the finger and thumb form a circle) is an insult in some cultures, signifying the person is worthless. Showing the sole of the foot is unacceptable in some cultures. Unless you know the person well, it is better to avoid gestures as a means of communication.

- Non-threatening use of body language. A pointing finger is threatening. A pat on the back or even a hug is a way of asserting power over someone. Open body language, where arms are relaxed at the sides, is neutral. Health and care workers should use non-threatening body language.

Figure 1.3 Non-threatening body language

- Personal space differs between cultures and between individuals. Some people feel uncomfortable if others are close. They may be described as 'standoffish' by someone who is comfortable with a smaller personal space.

Topic A.2 Alternative forms of communication

Communication varies with differing needs which may include:

- visual impairment
- hearing impairment
- learning disabilities and brain injury following accident or disease.

Forms of communication include:

- Braille and Braille software, for those with visual problems

Figure 1.4 Braille

- British Sign Language, for those with hearing difficulties
- finger spelling, for those with hearing difficulties
- text messaging, which is increasingly useful for many
- Bliss symbols and other picture systems to aid communication, for those with learning disabilities
- Makaton, which uses signs and symbols to aid communication, may help those with learning difficulties

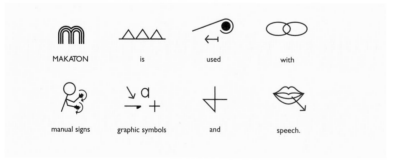

Figure 1.5 Makaton

- objects of reference such as a favourite toy may remind a child of home; family photographs may help someone with dementia to communicate.

Figure 1.6 Looking at a photo album can help to communicate with someone with dementia

People who may support communication include:

- interpreters for speech, for example from spoken English to BSL
- translators for the written word or documents
- advocates to speak on behalf of the persons who cannot speak for themselves.

Communication may be helped through technology. It may be basic technology using a notebook as a communication passport, a record of a person's communication methods to help when individuals cannot communicate for themselves independently.

Technological aids may be more complex: voice synthesisers help those who cannot speak; computer software reads the page aloud for those who cannot see; digital hearing aids help those with hearing loss.

Figure 1.7 Sign language interpreter

Knowledge recap questions

1. What elements form the communication cycle?

2. Name two forms of communication we use all the time.

3. Communication varies with individual needs. Name three needs that affect communication.

4. Which form of communication might you use with someone who has cerebral palsy?

Assessment guidance for Learning aim A

Scenario

You are volunteering at a local care centre. It could be a day centre or a residential centre for younger people with disabilities or for older people with disabilities. As part of the induction process, you are asked to investigate different forms of communication.

Research and present a series of case studies, then give a verbal presentation. Evidence presented verbally should be recorded. Detailed observation records or witness testimonies should be completed and retained for internal and external verification.

· ·

2A.P1 **Describe different forms of verbal and non-verbal communication.**

· ·

Assessor report: The command verb in the grading criteria is **describe**. In the learner's answers we would expect to see a detailed account of the forms of verbal and non-verbal communication skills, such as the use of non-discriminatory language and body language, which are used in health and social care.

✍ Learner answer

Communication is a two-way process. A message is sent by A and received by B who then responds with their message. There are some key elements in the cycle of communication and if any element is missing, communication can break down. First of all the sender – the person – starts the communication. They have a message to communicate. They decide the method of communication, whether verbal, written, signed, electronic, or telephone and send the message. The person who receives the message interprets it. They have to understand the message correctly otherwise communication has not worked. The receiver then has to give feedback, showing the sender that they have received and understood the message.**(a)**

In the first stage, when the sender has decided what message to send, they then decide whether to send the message verbally or non-verbally. These are the two main forms of communication. If they decide to use verbal communication, they must then think about how they will speak. It might be a whisper if they do not want everyone to hear, or it might be that they have to speak clearly for someone who has hearing loss.

The sender must use language that is age appropriate. If they are working with older people, they should be respectful and address the person in the way that person prefers, for example, Mr Singh, Miss Smith.

Language must be non-discriminatory. When Mary, the carer at the day centre, took details from Mr Singh, she asked what his first name was, not his Christian name, because he is not Christian. She did the same with Miss Smith because a carer should not discriminate. First name is a term that everyone can use.

Mary used an appropriate pace, tone and pitch. Mr Singh has dementia and English is not his first language so she slowed down the pace at which she spoke, used an encouraging tone and pitched her voice at the right level for him to hear.

She also used active listening skills, asking questions and nodding in agreement when he explained that it was difficult for him to remember things. This shows she is receiving and interpreting the message.

Mary used non-verbal communication skills. She sat with Mr Singh and leaned forward a little. Her posture showed she was interested in what he had to say. Her facial expressions showed patience when he could not find the words he needed and she kept eye contact to a brief glance, aware that in his culture women do not usually make eye contact with men. She sat close enough for him to hear but far enough away to respect his personal space, at an angle, not facing him in a confrontational way. She kept her feet on the floor, aware that crossing her legs was a defensive gesture, and also aware that she did not want to expose the bottom of her shoe, which he might find offensive.**(b)**

Assessor report: The learner has made a good start in describing different forms of verbal and non-verbal communication.

Assessor report – overall

What is good about this assessment evidence?

The learner starts by explaining a communication cycle and the key elements of such a cycle **(a)**. They then give a detailed account of verbal and non-verbal communication when communicating with a person from a different culture to their own. **(b)**

What could be improved about this assessment evidence?

It would be good to include a case study where there is communication with someone from a different age group and different ability.

2A.P2 **Describe different forms of alternative communication for different needs, using examples from health and social care.**

Assessor report: The command verb in the grading criteria is **describe**. In the learner's answers we would expect to see alternative forms of communication used for people who are visually impaired, hearing-impaired or have learning disabilities. Learners could use examples of alternative forms of communication they have used in a health and social care setting, or alternative forms of communication used across different settings.

The work for P1 would also be required.

 Learner answer

Alternative communication for people who are visually impaired

Jack (not his real name) attends a day centre for older people with visual impairment. He has lost his sight in the last few years. I worked with Jack when I was on placement. He had learned to use a computer before he lost his sight and he used e-mail to keep in touch with his son in Australia. When his eyesight started failing he felt sad because he felt he would not be able to communicate with his son so often. His son uses a mobile and telephone calls are expensive.

At the centre we had an IT specialist who found a programme that allowed Jack to dictate his e-mails and it would also read the ones he received out loud to him. Apple Mac have a programme called VoiceOver designed specifically for people with low vision or no vision **(c)**. Jack can magnify the screen up to 20 times and can get audio information when he has reached the end of a menu. Jack can even use a Braille keyboard with his computer. There are other speech recognition programmes available too where you just speak and the words appear on the screen. It also reads them back. Jack is busy finding out what is available.

Assessor report: The learner has made a good start in describing alternative communication for people who have a visual impairment. **(c)** They have included an example from a health and social care setting. The learner now needs to describe forms of alternative communication for other needs, including examples for each need.

Alternative communication for people who are hearing-impaired

Sally is in her late sixties and her hearing is not as good as it used to be. She attends a day centre once a week, for the company, but finds it difficult to hear conversations because of the background noise. She has a hearing aid but finds it difficult to manage. At the day centre Jess, one of the volunteers, showed Sally how to use SMS and now Sally communicates with her grandchildren by text.

Alternative communication for people who have learning disabilities

Josh has profound and multiple learning disabilities. Charlie is a volunteer at the residential unit where Josh lives. She tries to find out the best way to communicate with Josh. He likes his bright red feeding beaker so she shows it to him and then gives him a drink.

Assessor report: The learner has given a good description of alternative communication for people who are hearing-impaired and has included a good example from a health and social care setting. Although they have mentioned alternative communication for those who have learning disabilities, the description is limited.

Assessor report – overall

What is good about this assessment evidence?

The learner gives an example of alternative communication for people with hearing impairment, visual impairment and for people with learning difficulties.

What could be improved about this assessment evidence?

The learner needs to include a similar level of description for people with learning disabilities as they have done for those with visual and hearing impairments. It would be good to see a range of examples for each type of need, rather than just one.

2A.M1 Explain the advantages and disadvantages of different forms of communication used, with reference to a one-to-one and a group interaction.

Assessor report: The command verb in the grading criteria is **explain**. In the learner's answers we would expect them to provide details of the advantages and disadvantages of non-verbal, verbal, alternative forms of communication used referring to a one-to-one and group interaction in health and social care. They would need to give reasons and/or evidence to support the arguments being made.

The work for P1 and P2 would also be required.

✍ Learner answer

Non-verbal communication has several advantages. It can be used in a noisy place, or across a crowded room. Eye contact and a smile can help a nervous patient relax while waiting in a busy clinic or emergency department. In one-to-one situations, it can help communication. For example, when a person is telling the carer their past history, being seated with both feet on the floor, relaxed open body language, leaning forward with arms uncrossed, shows the person they are being listened to **(a)**. In group interaction non-verbal communication is also useful. In a care home, an activity co-ordinator can glance around a group, with a friendly smile, making eye contact and putting residents at ease before they start a remembering activity **(b)**.

Non-verbal communication also has disadvantages. It cannot convey a complex message and at times non-verbal communication can be misunderstood. In one-to-one situations, a person with learning disabilities may think the carer who listens so attentively and smiles at her wants a personal relationship, when all he is trying to do is to put her at her ease **(a)**. In group interaction, non-verbal communication may not be able to reach everyone, and one person may feel left out if the group leader does not give them equal eye contact. If a person in the group activity is from a different culture they may not understand the same meaning that everyone else does. In some cultures, men and women do not sit together, so a female carer sitting with a male patient in his room might be misinterpreted **(b)**.

Assessor report: The learner has made a good start in explaining advantages and disadvantages of non-verbal communication. They have made reference to both one-to-one (a) and group interactions (b) to support their explanation. The learner now needs to explain the advantages and disadvantages of verbal and alternative communication.

✍ Learner answer

Verbal communication has several advantages. It is useful for complex communication, for example, a doctor discussing a diagnosis with a patient in a one-to-one situation will use language as the main means of communication. Verbal communication is also useful in group situations such as an antenatal class, where a midwife gives information and parents-to-be want to ask questions.

Verbal communication also has disadvantages. The doctor discussing a diagnosis with a patient and the midwife running an antenatal class may use complicated or technical language which the listener does not understand. Someone who has a hearing impairment may find it difficult to hear what is said, both in one-to-one situations and in group situations. Those who do not speak English will not understand what is being said whether in a one-to-one situation or group situation. A carer advising Mr Malik, who is diabetic, about his diet will only get the message across if they speak the same language as he does. A health visitor advising a group of Yemeni parents about a child's diet will need to be able to communicate in the Yemeni dialect of Arabic if they are to be understood.

Assessor report: The learner has provided a good explanation of advantages and disadvantages of verbal communication for both one-to-one and group interactions. They have not explained the advantages and disadvantages of alternative forms of communication.

What is good about this assessment evidence?

The learner explains some advantages and some disadvantages of non-verbal and verbal communication. They give examples from health and social care to support what they say.

What could be improved about this assessment evidence?

The learner should complete their answer by considering the advantages of alternative forms of communication in one-to-one situations and in group interaction. They should also consider the disadvantages of alternative forms of communication in one-to-one situations and in group interaction.

(2A.D1) **Assess the effectiveness of different forms of communication for service users with different needs.**

● ●

Assessor report: The command verb in the grading criteria is **assess**. They should give careful consideration to at least five different forms of communication, and at least one of these must be an alternative form of communication. They should assess the effectiveness of different forms of communication for service users with different needs. The work for 2A.P1 and 2A.P2 would also be required. To avoid unnecessary repetition, the learner aiming for distinction should cover the distinction point, building on examples used in the merit point.

Distinction points are added in **bold** *in this example.*

 Learner answer

Non-verbal communication has several advantages. It can be used in a noisy place, across a crowded room. Eye contact and a smile can help a nervous patient relax while waiting in a busy clinic or emergency department. In one-to-one situations, it can help communication. For example, when a person is telling the carer their past history, being seated with both feet on the floor, relaxed open body language, leaning forward with arms uncrossed, shows the person they are being listened to. In group interaction non-verbal communication is useful. In a care home, an activity co-ordinator can glance around a group, with a friendly smile, making eye contact and putting residents at ease before they start a remembering activity.

Non-verbal communication also has disadvantages. It cannot convey a complex message and at times non-verbal communication can be misunderstood.

In one-to-one situations, a person with learning disabilities may think the carer who listens so attentively and smiles at her wants a personal relationship, when all he is trying to do is to put her at her ease. In group interaction, non-verbal communication may not be able to reach everyone, and one person may feel left out if the group leader does not give them equal eye contact. If a person in the group activity is from a different culture, they may not understand the same meaning that everyone else does. In some cultures, men and women do not sit together, so a female carer sitting with a male patient in his room might be misinterpreted.

Eye contact has both advantages and disadvantages. It is quick, can be used in noisy places and crowded environments and is useful when communicating with those with hearing impairments but it is difficult to reach everyone in a group by eye contact alone (a). Too much eye contact can be aggressive and threatening. It is not useful when communicating with people with visual impairments and should be used with caution when working with people with learning difficulties to avoid misunderstandings (b) (c). Eye contact is probably most effective when working one to one, or with small groups who can see the person communicating.

Posture, for example, not crossing arms or legs, being at the same level as the person you are communicating with, and having an open posture has advantages and disadvantages. It can put people at ease but should be used with caution when working with people with learning disabilities as they may have difficulty in understanding professional boundaries (c). Part of a care worker's role is to help a person with learning disabilities socialise, which may involve taking them as part of a group for a meal in a pub. It is difficult for someone with learning disabilities and uncertain social skills to know where the boundary is between carer and friend. The carer may think their posture shows friendliness and support but the care receiver may think it means closeness. A more closed posture could be used to indicate distance but if someone has poor social skills they may not pick up on this signal (c). Posture has a further disadvantage in that it works only when a person has sight. It is not useful when communicating with people with visual impairments (b). Posture is most effective when communicating with sighted people who can understand social signals. It is least effective when communicating with those who cannot see and those who do not understand the significance of posture.

Assessor report: The learner has explained advantages and disadvantages of non-verbal communication. They have then built upon the answer they provided for 2A.M1 and gone on to assess the effectiveness of two forms of non-verbal communication (eye contact and posture). They have assessed how effective these two forms of communication are for service users with three different needs (those with hearing impairments (a), visual impairments (b) and/or learning difficulties (c)). They now need to assess the effectiveness of three different forms of communication. At least one of these must be an alternative form of communication.

Learner answer

Verbal communication has several advantages. It is useful for complex communication, for example, a doctor discussing a diagnosis with a patient in a one-to-one situation will use language as the main means of communication. Verbal communication is also useful in group situations such as an antenatal class, where a midwife gives information and parents-to-be want to ask questions.

Verbal communication also has disadvantages. The doctor discussing a diagnosis with a patient and the midwife running an antenatal class may use complicated or technical language which the listener does not understand. Someone who has a hearing impairment may find it difficult to hear what is said, both in one-to-one situations and in group situations. Those who do not speak English will not understand what is being said whether in a one-to-one situation or group situation. A carer advising Mr Malik, who is diabetic, about his diet will only get the message across if they speak the same language as he does. A health visitor advising a group of Yemeni parents about a child's diet will need to be able to communicate in the Yemeni dialect of Arabic if they are to be understood.

Assessor report: The learner explained advantages and disadvantages of verbal communication in one-to-one and group interactions, but has not developed their work from 2A.M1 to assess the effectiveness of this form of communication.

Assessor report – overall

What is good about this assessment evidence?

The learner explains some advantages and disadvantages of non-verbal and verbal communication, using examples from health and social care they used for 2A.M1. They have extended this work to assess the effectiveness of two forms of non-verbal communication, eye contact and posture, when communicating with service users with hearing impairments, visual impairments and learning difficulties.

What could be improved about this assessment evidence?

As with their answer to 2A.M1, the learner needs to consider the advantages and disadvantages of alternative forms of communication in one-to-one situations and in group interaction. The learner has currently only assessed two different forms of communication. To achieve 2A.D1, at least five different forms of communication should be assessed, with at least one of these being an alternative form of communication. They should assess the effectiveness of different forms of communication for service users with different needs, such as those with a hearing impairment, or visual impairment or learning disabilities.

Learning aim B

Investigate barriers to communication in health and social care

UNIT 3 Effective Communication in Health and Social Care

Assessment criteria

2B.P3 Describe the barriers to communication in health and social care and their effects on service users.

2B.P4 Using examples, explain ways in which barriers to communication may be overcome and the benefits to service users of overcoming these barriers.

2B.M2 Explain how measures have been implemented to overcome barriers to communication, with reference to a selected case.

2B.D2 Evaluate the effectiveness of measures taken to remove barriers to communication, with reference to a selected case.

Topic B.1 Barriers to communication and how to overcome them

Barriers to communication

Studied ☐

Barriers to communication include the following:

- Environmental barriers such as poor lighting, badly arranged seating, external noise and lack of space.
- Physical barriers, for example sensory deprivation such as hearing or visual impairment, physical and mental illness.
- Language barriers.
- Having English as an additional language.
- Someone who uses British Sign Language will not be able to understand someone who uses spoken English.
- Speech difficulties and slang may cause barriers.

- Acronyms where a word is formed from initials, such as NHS for National Health Service, create a barrier because not everyone knows what the initials stand for.
- Colloquialisms or informal expressions such as 'kid' meaning child, or 'it's raining cats and dogs', can pose a barrier for those unfamiliar with those expressions.
- Words such as 'rhinopharyngitis' and 'acute coryza' are names for the common cold, but the jargon makes it difficult to understand what disorder is meant.
- Social isolation. This may lead to a lack of confidence or may be caused by a lack of confidence. Social isolation may follow on from intimidation, abuse or trauma. Whatever the cause of social isolation, it poses a barrier to communication.

Figure 2.1 Social isolation

Effects of barriers to communication

Studied ■

The effects of barriers on individuals are:

- Reduced access to health and social care services, as people may not understand how to get services they need.
- Poor quality of delivery of health and social care, as when someone reaches the surgery or hospital they may not understand where to go and what to do.
- Distress – not being able to get a service because of poor communication causes distress.
- Increased social issues, for example, a drug addict may not know that the doctor can help them get off drugs, and may resort to stealing to fund his habit. A woman who is depressed may not realise that she can get help, and may turn to alcohol and neglect her children because she did not know how to get help, due to poor communication.
- Increased ill health, which results if people do not know that care is available when they need it.

Overcoming barriers

Studied ■

We can overcome barriers by the use of:

- preferred method of communication
- preferred language
- adaptations to the physical environment such as changes to seating, lighting and soundproofing of rooms/windows
- effective non-verbal communication – positive posture, facial expressions and appropriate gestures.

Benefits when barriers are removed

Studied ■

The benefits to individuals when barriers are removed may be:

- increased access to health and social care
- improved quality of health and social care delivery
- reduction of emotional distress
- increased involvement in interactions
- raised levels of self-esteem
- reduced frustration.

Figure 2.2 Overcoming barriers

Knowledge recap questions

1. Name four barriers to communication.

2. Name five effects of barriers on individuals.

3. Give four ways of overcoming barriers.

4. Give six benefits to individuals when barriers are removed.

Assessment guidance for Learning aim B

Scenario

You are volunteering at a local care centre. It could be a day centre or a residential centre for younger people with disabilities or for older people with disabilities. As part of the induction process, you are asked to investigate barriers to communication in health and social care, their effects and how to overcome the barriers.

Research and present a series of case studies then give a PowerPoint presentation. For the merit and distinction you may need to write notes to accompany your slides to cover the depth of analysis and the evaluation. Evidence presented verbally should be recorded. All notes should be retained for internal and external verification.

2B.P3 **Describe the barriers to communication in health and social care and their effects on service users.**

Assessor report: The command verb in the grading criteria is **describe**. The learner should give a detailed description of four types of barriers to communication in health and social care and their effects on service users. Learners should refer to case studies or actual cases in the news.

✍ Learner answer

Barriers to communication are factors that break or interfere with the communication cycle described in 2A.P1. Barriers could be environmental, physical, due to language or they could be due to social isolation **(a)**.

Environmental barriers could be in the area around the person. Poor lighting and seating lining the wall rather than grouped to see others will form barriers to communication. External noise from traffic or nearby noise from an echoing hall could prevent people hearing what others are saying. Hard surfaces bounce noise rather than absorb it, so that someone with hearing impairment has difficulty in hearing the separate sounds of words as everything blends together into a buzzing noise. Lack of space can prevent people turning to have a chat or getting up and moving to be near friends.

Physical barriers may include sensory deprivation such as hearing or visual impairment. Those with hearing impairment may need to lip read, and cannot hear if a carer speaks behind them. It is no use asking Mrs Jones if she would like a cup of tea if she lip reads to communicate and is facing away from you **(b)**. Visual impairment can also be a barrier to communication. Mr Norton with poor eyesight may not see another person smile at him, or may not see a carer wave across a room to attract his attention **(b)**. Physical illness may make a person reluctant to move. If, for example, like Mrs Jones they have arthritis and painful joints, they will not want to walk across the room to sit near a friend at the day centre **(b)**. Mental illness is perhaps the most difficult barrier to overcome because there is no apparent reason for their failure to communicate. A person with arthritis may have a walking stick. A visually impaired person may have a guide dog or a white stick, but someone with depression has nothing to show they are ill. They may be labelled 'rude' if they do not respond when someone speaks to them. John lost his wife of forty years and lives alone. His depression makes it hard for him to talk to people at the day centre **(b)**.

Assessor report: The learner has made a good start by introducing the four different types of barriers to communication in their opening paragraph **(a)**. They have described environmental and physical barriers to communication and have given supporting examples from health and social care to show how these barriers effect service users. They now need to provide similar descriptions for language barriers and social isolation.

Language can be a barrier to communication. Some people with a hearing impairment from birth use British Sign Language. Others have English as an additional language. According to the census of 2011, in England and Wales, Polish is the second most spoken language after English and Welsh. While many Polish people speak very good English, in London there are over 100 languages spoken so many people have language barriers to communication. Mrs Khan attends a day centre but no one speaks her language so she cannot communicate with anyone there (c). Mary uses British Sign Language and has the same problem. She cannot understand what people are saying because no one else uses BSL (c).

Speech difficulties cause a barrier. Mr Norton is recovering from a stroke and still has difficulty speaking. It is hard for the staff at the centre to understand him (c).

Slang may cause barriers. Mrs Jones lip reads but when Sally, one of the carers, describes her boyfriend as 'wicked', Mrs Jones is confused (c).

Acronyms create a barrier because not everyone knows what the initials stand for. In the attendance book for Tuesday, Sally sees 'DNA' written against Mrs Jones's name (c). She asks the manager, who explains it stands for 'did not attend'.

Colloquialisms or informal expressions such as 'pinking it down' for 'raining heavily' confused Sally when she first heard one of the other carers say it (c).

Jargon can pose a barrier, especially for those unfamiliar with medical expressions. Sally was told that Mr Norton was hemiplegic and had dysphagia. She had to ask what these terms meant. The manager explained that hemiplegia was weakness on one side following his stroke and dysphagia meant difficulty swallowing (c). It was important that Sally understood this as Mr Norton could easily choke on his lunch if food was not cut up for him. Weakness on one side meant his balance was uncertain and he could fall if he stood up to go to the toilet.

Social isolation is the fourth factor that may be a barrier to communication.

Assessor report: The learner has described language barriers to communication and has given supporting examples for each barrier (c). They have not described social isolation and its effects on service users.

Assessor report – overall

What is good about this assessment evidence?

The learner described environmental, physical and language barriers to communication. They have supported each description of a barrier with an example.

What could be improved about this assessment evidence?

The fourth factor, social isolation, should be described and a supporting example given. The effects of barriers on individuals, for example, reduced access to health and social care services, poor quality of delivery of health and social care, distress, increased social issues, and increased ill health should be included to complete the point.

TOWER HAMLETS COLLEGE
POPLAR HIGH STREET
LONDON
E14 0AF

2B.P4 **Using examples, explain ways in which barriers to communication may be overcome and the benefits to service users of overcoming these barriers.**

Assessor report: The command verb in the grading criteria is **explain**. Learners should provide details and give reasons and examples to explain how each type of barrier can be overcome and explain the benefits to service users of overcoming these barriers.

In 2B.P3 four barriers were identified. They were environmental, physical, language and social isolation. How these can be overcome and the benefits to service users of overcoming these barriers are the focus of this next section.

✍ Learner answer

Care workers can overcome barriers by using the method of communication the service user prefers, such as BSL for Mary, or learning some words of Urdu to communicate with Mrs Khan **(a)**. This takes time but shows service users that their communication is respected.

Adaptations to the physical environment such as changes to seating will help Mr Norton who has poor eyesight and mobility problems see others and be near enough to talk **(a)**. Better lighting **(a)** will help Mrs Jones lip read and soundproofing rooms and windows will cut out external noise, making it easier for everyone to hear in the day centre.

The volunteers and care workers can practise effective non-verbal communication – positive posture such as sitting down to talk with John who is depressed and isolated, instead of leaning over him. Using appropriate facial expressions such as smiling across the room to Mary and Mrs Jones is effective in overcoming barriers **(a)**. Using appropriate gestures they can ask Mary, who is deaf, and Mrs Khan, who does not speak English, if they want a drink or tell them that the taxi is here to take them home **(a)**.

The benefits to individuals when barriers are removed can be seen in each example.

By learning to communicate with Mrs Khan and with Mary, carers can find out if their needs are being met by the day centre, or if there is anything else that can be done **(b)**. Mrs Khan has problems with her spectacles and may need to see an optician, which can be arranged through the day centre. By spending time talking with Mr Norton they find that he needs a chiropodist to cut his toenails **(b)**. These are just a few examples of how removing barriers can increase access to health and social care.

Assessor report: The learner has made a good start in explaining how barriers to communication can be overcome and has given supporting examples **(a)**. They have briefly mentioned the benefit of finding out users' needs in overcoming these barriers **(b)**.

Assessor report – overall

What is good about this assessment evidence?

The learner has explained how each barrier can be overcome and has supported each description with an example, linking to previous case studies from 2B.P3 to avoid repetition.

What could be improved about this assessment evidence?

The learner needs to further explain the benefits to service users of overcoming the barriers they have explained. They should explain, with examples, how overcoming barriers leads to improved quality of health and social care delivery, reduction of emotional distress, increased involvement in interactions, raised levels of self-esteem and reduced frustration.

(2B.M2) Explain how measures have been implemented to overcome barriers to communication, with reference to a selected case.

Assessor report: The command verb in the grading criteria is **explain**. Learners should develop their responses for 2B.P3 and 2B.P4 to explain how measures have been implemented in a health and social care setting to overcome barriers. Learners can build on evidence already presented or refer to a local case study, or to measures that have been implemented at a national level.

✎ **Learner answer**

Care workers in both health care and social care need skills in communication. At the day centre, all the staff have regular training and some of this covers aspects of communication. Two of the staff have already gained care qualifications at an advanced level, and the others are studying for care qualifications. In these qualifications they learn about verbal and non-verbal communication. The manager is keen to support staff training as inspectors will be looking at training records for staff. Two of the staff have undertaken training in using basic British Sign Language. One is learning Urdu at evening class so that she can communicate better with Mrs Khan.

At a staff meeting the team considered how they could adapt the physical environment to improve communication. They decided to make changes to seating. Instead of having all the chairs round the edge of the room they grouped them in threes and fours so that people could see each other. Improved lighting was requested and approved but soundproofing the doors, rooms and windows was not approved by the management. Instead of soundproofing, someone suggested having more soft furnishings such as table covers and cushions to absorb noise.

The day centre uses care plans to identify the communication needs of individuals. Previously this information was held by the manager but not divulged to carers. One of the ways to overcome communication barriers suggested at the team meeting was to share this information.

Assessor report: The learner has made a good start in explaining how measures have been implemented in a health and social care setting to overcome barriers.

Assessor report – overall

What is good about this assessment evidence?

The learner builds on previous work and explains how barriers have been overcome in a day centre.

What could be improved about this assessment evidence?

It would be good to include more explanation of how to overcome barriers and ensure effective non-verbal communication such as positive posture, facial expressions and appropriate gestures. At the moment the learner has said training is the answer, but a more detailed explanation of how this happens would be better. The learner could include getting feedback from service users on how they feel communication could be improved.

2B.D2 **Evaluate the effectiveness of measures taken to remove barriers to communication, with reference to a selected case.**

Assessor report: The command verb in the grading criteria is **evaluate**. Learners should bring together all the information and review it to form a conclusion and evaluate how effective the measures were in removing barriers. Their answer to 2B.D2 should build on the work they have completed for 2B.M2.

Distinction work is included here in **bold**.

✍ Learner answer

Care workers in both health care and social care need skills in communication. At the day centre, all the staff have regular training and some of this covers aspects of communication. Two of the staff have already gained care qualifications at an advanced level, and the others are studying for care qualifications. In these qualifications they learn about verbal and non-verbal communication. The manager is keen to support staff training as inspectors will be looking at training records for staff.

In theory, training is a good way to overcome barriers but for it to be effective, it must be put into practice. Some of the carers see what they do for their care qualification as separate to ordinary work and do not put into practice what they have learned. The manager asks them what they have learned but they just say 'communication'. For those who put what they have learned into practice, training is effective in improving communication skills and removing barriers, but there are a few people for whom this is not effective. In conclusion, training is only partly effective in removing barriers to communication.

Two of the staff have undertaken training in using basic British Sign Language. One is learning Urdu at evening classes so that she can communicate better with Mrs Khan. **This way to overcome language barriers is partly effective. Both Mary and Mrs Khan feel happy that someone is trying to learn their language** but the carers learning BSL and Urdu know only a few words so cannot have a proper conversation with the service users. The main problem is that learning any language to be able to communicate well takes a long time. Again the effectiveness of this way to overcome barriers is limited.

At a staff meeting the team considered how they could adapt the physical environment to improve communication. They decided to make changes to seating. Instead of having all the chairs round the edge of the room they grouped them in threes and fours so that people could see each other. Improved lighting was requested and approved but soundproofing the doors, rooms and windows was not approved by the management. Instead of soundproofing, someone suggested having more soft furnishings such as table covers and cushions to absorb noise.

Re-arranging the furniture so that people sit in small groups proved to be very effective. John found that helping Mr Norton and watching that he did not fall took his mind off his own problems and helped lift the depression. Mary and Mrs Jones sat together and Mary taught Mrs Jones some simple BSL. Mrs Khan sat with them and learned some too. They became friends and started a sewing circle to make cushion covers for the new cushions.

Assessor report: The learner has made a good start in evaluating the effectiveness of measures taken to remove barriers to communication, using a selected case.

Assessor report – overall

What is good about this assessment evidence?

The learner builds on previous work and uses evaluative language, such as very effective, or partly effective, to come to a conclusion.

What could be improved about this assessment evidence?

In addition to the feedback for 2B.M2, the learner should complete an evaluation of effectiveness of remaining measures not yet covered (sharing care plans with carers).

Learning aim C

Communicate effectively in health and social care

Assessment criteria

2C.P5 Demonstrate communication skills through interactions in health and social care, describing their effects.

2C.M3 Select and demonstrate communication skills through interactions in health and social care, explaining their effectiveness.

2C.D3 Select and demonstrate communication skills through one-to-one and group interactions in health and social care, evaluating their effectiveness and making recommendations for improvement.

Topic C.1 Communicating with groups and individuals

We use the same skills when communicating with groups as we use when we communicate in a one-to-one situation. We just need to adapt or modify the skills to suit the situation.

Communication skills

Studied

The communication skills we use are:

- Active listening, showing that we are listening by nodding or murmuring agreement.
- Body language is open, not defensive.
- Facial expression shows interest, not boredom.
- Eye contact is appropriate – not staring but not looking over the person's shoulder as though there is something more interesting across the room.
- Use of appropriate language that they can understand.
- Tone of voice – usually a neutral tone is best, not emotional.
- Pace of speech – this should suit the listener. If you speak too fast they will miss information and if you speak too slowly they will be bored and stop listening.
- Proximity – too close is uncomfortable, too far away and they cannot hear.

- Clarifying by checking back, for example, 'Do you mean you want to try dressing yourself before we help?' and repeating, 'Did you say, "I want to dress myself?"'

Figure 3.1 Active listening

Effectiveness of communication

Studied

Communication is effective only when it works. Sometimes it works and sometimes it does not. We can improve the effectiveness of communication by:

- Reflecting on skills used: ask what happened, what worked, what did not work, what would I change to improve it next time?
- Selecting appropriate communication methods for different service users.
- Making recommendations for improvement and carrying out the recommendations.

Knowledge recap questions

1. Name ten skills we use when communicating one to one or with groups.

2. Give examples of four questions to ask when reflecting back on an activity.

3. What do we mean by 'selecting an appropriate communication method'?

4. Why is it not enough just to make recommendations?

Assessment guidance for Learning aim C

Scenario

You are volunteering at the day centre which Mr Norton attends. He has had a stroke and has difficulty speaking. He is also weak down one side and needs help to walk with his walking frame. He has poor eyesight.

Take the role of a care worker and discuss Mr Norton's care with him to check that he is satisfied with the care and whether any changes need to be made. You will be observed and assessed on this. Later in a group situation you will need to present your findings and discuss this with the rest of the team.

2C.P5 **Demonstrate communication skills through interactions in health and social care, describing their effects.**

Assessor report: The command verb in the grading criteria is **demonstrate**. Learners must show their communication skills through interactions which could be recorded. Learners should produce a checklist for the observations as part of a class activity and produce notes, which could support them when producing their evidence for 2C.P5.

Learner answer

Checklist for communication skills. Observer to tick as achieved and add comments as needed.

Communication skills	Comments
Greet the service user	
Introduce yourself	
Explain reason for interaction – to plan care	
Non-verbal communication skills	
Eye contact	
Facial expressions	
Posture – appropriate	
Personal space	
Body language	
Gestures	

Assessor report: The learner produced a checklist for the observer to use, but has not included verbal communication such as clear speech, selection of appropriate language, use or avoidance of slang and regional words as appropriate, avoidance of jargon, age-appropriate language, pace, tone and pitch, non-discriminatory use of language and active listening skills. They also need to produce some notes to support the checklist.

Notes

I was nervous and forgot to introduce myself but I did say 'Hello Mr Norton' and explained that we were going to look at his needs and review his care plan.

Mr Norton has poor eyesight and he cannot turn himself in his chair easily so I made sure I stood in front of him where he could see me.

I said, 'Do you mind if I sit down?' and gestured to an empty chair near to him so he could understand what I meant. I thought he might be worried so I smiled to reassure him. When I sat down, I sat just to one side where the light fell on my face so he could see me better and glanced across at him – not staring, but just enough to make eye contact.

I had a clipboard and rested it on my knees. I think that may have been a bit defensive because I was nervous, but at least I did not cross my arms or cross my legs. Anyway when we got talking, I put it to one side and just listened. I had gone there with a list of things I wanted to check but when he started talking about his past life it was so interesting that I forgot to make notes. I was leaning forward, listening to all the stories of when he was young. I did not know he had had such an adventurous life. Listening to his life story really helped me understand him better. I know now he is very independent and does not want to be fussed over. If he wants help he will ask, especially when it comes to getting dressed.

At times it was hard to understand him when he spoke quickly, but I checked out that I understood him by repeating it back to him slowly. He nodded to show I had understood correctly.

Assessor report: The learner has made a good start in describing their interaction and the communication skills used. However, they have not included notes on the different examples of verbal communication, which should have been included in the checklist.

Assessor report – overall

What is good about this assessment evidence?

The learner produced a checklist for the observer and has made notes immediately after the interaction to capture the skills they used.

What could be improved about this assessment evidence?

The checklist should be amended to include the aspects of verbal communication mentioned. Notes should also reflect on these aspects of communication skills.

2C.M3 Select and demonstrate communication skills through interactions in health and social care, explaining their effectiveness.

Assessor report: The command verbs in the grading criteria are **select** and **demonstrate**. Learners should select and apply communication skills in at least two different situations in health and social care. These could be one-to-one or group, formal or informal, with colleagues or service users. Learners should explain the effectiveness of the skills they demonstrated.

✍ Learner answer

The two situations I will be describing are a formal team meeting which involves group interaction with colleagues, and a one-to-one informal interaction with a service user.

Both situations require verbal communication skills such as clear speech, selection of appropriate language, avoidance of slang jargon. They need age-appropriate language, suitable pace, tone and pitch, non-discriminatory language and active listening skills. Both situations also require non-verbal communication skills, such as a suitable posture which is positive and non defensive. Facial expressions should match the conversation, and eye contact should be sufficient to maintain interaction without being aggressive. The use of touch and personal space should be considered carefully as should gestures. Body language should be non-threatening and personal space should be carefully considered.

Note – a checklist should be completed by an observer to accompany learner notes.

Communication skills		Comments
Introduce yourself	√	
Explain reason for interaction	√	
Non-verbal communication skills		
Eye contact	√	
Facial expressions	√	
Posture – appropriate	√	
Personal space	√	The room was small for the number of people.
Body language	√	Once the learner crossed their arms but then uncrossed them.
Gestures	√	
Verbal communication		
Clear speech	√	Most of the time.
Appropriate language	√	Good explanation of technical terms.
Pace, tone and pitch	√	Spoke slowly, serious tone, and lower pitch than their usual squeaky voice.
Non-discriminatory use of language	√	Excellent use of non-discriminatory language.
Active listening skills	√	Leaning forward, nodding in agreement, showing interest in the discussion that followed her presentation.

Assessor report: The learner made a good start by identifying appropriate communication skills for the situation and including a completed checklist for one situation (a formal team meeting). They now need to provide supporting notes and explain their effectiveness, as well as a completed checklist and notes for the one-to-one informal interaction with a service user.

Learner answer

Notes

Mr Norton (not his real name) has had a stroke and has difficulty speaking. He is also weak down one side and needs help to walk with his walking frame. He has poor eyesight. I was asked to plan the care for Mr Norton and present the plan for discussion with the rest of the team.

There were about eight people at the meeting held in the manager's office. I had to present my plan as the first item. I had copies and distributed them at the meeting so people could follow what I was talking about. I know I have a quiet voice and had to make sure I spoke clearly so everyone could hear. I had to speak slower than I usually do, with a confident tone and pitch my voice a bit lower than usual because when I am nervous I can get a bit shrill. I had to use formal language, so had to find out and use the correct term for weakness on one side, which is hemiplegia. Difficulty in swallowing is dysphagia, another formal term I had to use. Although I have heard other people use the term 'geriatric' for older people, I did not use it because it is discriminatory. I referred to Mr Norton as an older person.

It is a small room and was a bit crowded. I felt uncomfortable as we were squashed up so tried to limit my use of gestures because I use my hands a lot when talking. I was nervous and aware that I was at one point standing with my arms crossed, which is defensive, so I made a conscious effort to relax, uncross my arms and make eye contact with people while presenting my plan. I do slouch so I tried to stand up straight to show I was taking it seriously. I think because I was nervous, I felt tempted to smile too much. After I presented the plan, the team discussed it and asked me some questions which made me think more about details. I was really interested in what they had to say, and showed it by leaning forward, and nodding in agreement.

I think my communication skills were effective because I presented the plan and everybody seemed to understand what I was saying. At one point I had to speak up because one of the carers could not hear, and I had to explain 'dysphagia' and 'hemiplegia' to her **(a)**.

Assessor report: The learner has included notes which support the checklist for the formal team meeting and demonstrate communication skills. They have included a brief explanation of their effectiveness (a). The effectiveness of each individual skill should be explained, rather than a general explanation given.

Assessor report – overall

What is good about this assessment evidence?

The learner has included a checklist to support their notes. Appropriate skills were clearly demonstrated.

What could be improved about this assessment evidence?

The effectiveness of each individual skill should be explained, rather than a general explanation given. A second interaction is needed which should be one-to-one, and the effectiveness of these skills should also be explained.

2C.D3 Select and demonstrate communication skills through one-to-one and group interactions in health and social care, evaluating their effectiveness and making recommendations for improvement.

Assessor report: The command verbs in the grading criteria are **select**, **demonstrate**, **evaluate** and **make recommendations**. Learners should have selected and applied communication skills in two different situations in health and social care for 2C.M3. These could be one-to-one or group, formal or informal, with colleagues or service users. They should have explained the effectiveness of the skills they demonstrated. For 2C.D3 they need to add to this work. As part of their evaluation, learners need to make recommendations for improving their use of communication skills.

This learner answer shows how the distinction point (in **bold***) can be included.*

✍ Learner answer

The two situations I will be describing are a formal team meeting which involves group interaction with colleagues, and a one-to-one informal interaction with a service user.

When selecting skills, it is important to recognise which are appropriate for each situation. Both situations require verbal communication skills such as clear speech, selection of appropriate language, avoidance of slang and jargon. They need age-appropriate language, suitable pace, tone and pitch, non-discriminatory language and active listening skills. Both situations also require non-verbal communication skills such as a suitable posture which is positive and non-defensive. Facial expressions should match the conversation, and eye contact should be sufficient to maintain interaction without being aggressive. The use of touch and personal space should be considered carefully as should gestures. Body language should be non-threatening and personal space should be carefully considered.

Note – an observer should complete and sign a checklist to accompany learner notes. This could meet the requirement for demonstration.

Communication skills		Comments
Introduce yourself	√	
Explain reason for interaction	√	
Non-verbal communication skills		
Eye contact	√	
Facial expressions	√	
Posture – appropriate	√	
Personal space	√	*The room was small for the number of people.*
Body language	√	*Once the learner crossed their arms but then uncrossed them.*
Gestures	√	
Verbal communication		
Clear speech	√	*Most of the time.*
Appropriate language	√	*Good explanation of technical terms.*
Pace, tone and pitch	√	*Spoke slowly, serious tone, and lower pitch than their usual squeaky voice.*
Non-discriminatory use of language	√	*Excellent use of non-discriminatory language.*
Active listening skills	√	*Leaning forward, nodding in agreement, showing interest in the discussion that followed her presentation.*

Notes

Mr Norton (not his real name) has had a stroke and has difficulty speaking. He is also weak down one side and needs help to walk with his walking frame. He has poor eyesight. I was asked to plan the care for Mr Norton and present the plan for discussion with the rest of the team.

Explanation of skills

There were about eight people at the meeting held in the manager's office. I had to present my plan as the first item. I had copies and distributed them at the meeting so people could follow what I was talking about. I know I have a quiet voice and had to make sure I spoke clearly so everyone could hear. I had to speak slower than I usually do, with a confident tone and pitch my voice a bit lower than usual because when I am nervous I can get a bit shrill. I had to use formal language, so had to find out and use the correct term for weakness on one side, which is hemiplegia. Difficulty in swallowing is dysphagia, another formal term I had to use. Although I have heard other people use the term 'geriatric' for older people, I did not use it because it is discriminatory. I referred to Mr Norton as an older person.

It is a small room and was a bit crowded. I felt uncomfortable as we were squashed up so tried to limit my use of gestures because I use my hands a lot when talking. I was nervous and aware that I was at one point standing with my arms crossed, which is defensive, so I made a conscious effort to relax, uncross my arms and make eye contact with people while presenting my plan. I do slouch so I tried to stand up straight to show I was taking it seriously. I think because I was nervous, I felt tempted to smile too much. After I presented the plan, the team discussed it and asked me some questions which made me think more about details. I was really interested in what they had to say, and showed it by leaning forward, and nodding in agreement.

Effectiveness

I think my communication skills were effective because I presented the plan and everybody seemed to understand what I was saying. At one point I had to speak up because one of the carers could not hear, and I had to explain 'dysphagia' and 'hemiplegia' to her. Skills that were used most effectively were the selection of appropriate language and the pace and tone.

I was effective in communicating my interest when I leaned forward and nodded in agreement. I was careful to select my words and avoid discriminatory language. I think this worked because no one seemed offended by what I said.

I think I was less effective at times with my body language because I was nervous and crossed my arms creating a barrier between myself and the listeners. Another aspect of the situation was that everybody was squashed into a small office. They could not spread out and this closeness could have been a distraction for some people.

Recommendations for improvement

(Distinction point.)

Next time I have to talk to a group I will check first to make sure there is enough room. Although this is not about my own communication skills it affects what the listener receives. I will also prepare my information so that I do not have to keep looking at my papers and can spend time making eye contact and establishing a rapport with each person.

I need to practise a relaxed posture. I will spend a few minutes visualising a similar scene and associate feeling comfortable with it, so I will practise this for a few minutes each day so that I can adopt a relaxed posture when I need it.

Assessor report: The learner has selected appropriate communication skills for the group situation. They have a signed observer checklist to support their notes for each interaction. Appropriate skills were clearly demonstrated and the effectiveness of separate skills is evaluated. The learner has made recommendations for improvement (shown in bold) on the group interaction. They now need to provide similar work for a one-to-one situation with a service user.

TOWER HAMLETS COLLEGE
POPLAR HIGH STREET
LONDON
E14 0AF

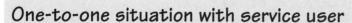

One-to-one situation with service user

Mr Norton has had a stroke and has difficulty speaking. He is also weak down one side and needs help to walk with his walking frame. He has poor eyesight.

Skills selected to demonstrate are verbal and also non-verbal. As Mr Norton has poor eyesight it is important for me to have clear speech and use language he can understand. Non-verbal communication such as gestures may need to be clear and I will need to make sure that I sit close enough for him to hear me without invading his personal space. I will also need to check that I am on the side where he can see me best as he cannot turn easily due to his weakness. I will need to check that the pace is right.

Checklist for communication skills. Observer has ticked if achieved and added comments as needed.

Communication skills		Comments
Introduce yourself	√	*Learner said who she was.*
Explain reason for interaction	√	*Explained the reason for the discussion.*
Non-verbal communication skills		
Eye contact	√	*Good eye contact.*
Facial expressions	√	*Clear facial expressions that matched what she said.*
Posture – appropriate	√	*Relaxed open posture, facing him. She also checked the lighting was good so he could see her.*
Personal space	√	*Made sure he was comfortable.*
Body language	√	*Leaning forward, nodding.*
Gestures	√	*Very few used but those that were used were clear.*
Verbal communication		
Clear speech	√	*All the time.*
Appropriate language	√	*Avoided technical terms.*
Pace, tone and pitch	√	*Spoke slowly, friendly tone.*
Non-discriminatory use of language	√	*Excellent use of non-discriminatory language.*
Active listening skills	√	*Leaning forward, nodding in agreement, showing interest in what he had to say.*

Notes

I was nervous and almost forgot to introduce myself but remembered just in time. I said 'Hello Mr Norton' and explained that we wanted to check that he was happy with the care and that we were doing all we could to help him become independent again.

Mr Norton has poor eyesight and he cannot turn himself in his chair easily so I made sure I was in front of him where he could see me then I said, 'Do you mind if I sit down?' and gestured to an empty chair near to him so he could understand what I meant. I thought he might be worried so I smiled to reassure him. When I sat down, I sat just to one side where the light fell on my face so he could see me better and glanced across at him – not staring, but just enough to make eye contact.

I had a clipboard and rested it on my knees. I think that may have been a bit defensive because I was nervous, but at least I did not cross my arms or cross my legs. Anyway when we got talking, I put it to one side and just listened. I had gone there with a list of things I wanted to check but when he started talking about his past life it was so interesting that I forgot to make notes. I was leaning forward, listening to all the stories of when he was young. I did not know he had had such an adventurous life. He had been in the Navy as a young man and had travelled a lot. Later he ran his own company.

Listening to his life story really helped me understand him better. I know now he is very independent and does not want to be fussed over. He wants to try to do things for himself even if it takes a long time. If he wants help he will ask, especially when it comes to getting dressed.

At times it was hard to understand him, but I checked out that I understood him by repeating it back to him slowly. He nodded to show I had understood correctly.

Effectiveness

Sitting near him in a good light so that he could see my face was effective. Communicating at the right pace, giving him time to speak was effective. My posture and body language showed that I was making an effort to understand him which again was effective.

I think I could have been more effective when using gestures to reinforce what I was saying. Although he has poor eyesight, he can see and a few more gestures would have helped. I also abandoned the idea of taking notes because that was a barrier and distracted me from what he was saying.

Assessor report: The learner has selected appropriate communication skills and has included a signed observer checklist. They have demonstrated appropriate skills and explained their effectiveness. They have not made any recommendations for improvement.

Assessor report – overall

What is good about this assessment evidence?

The learner has a signed observer checklist to support their notes for each interaction. Appropriate skills were clearly demonstrated and the effectiveness of separate skills was assessed. The learner has made recommendations for improvement on the group interaction.

What could be improved about this assessment evidence?

Recommendations for improvement are needed for the second interaction, the one-to-one situation.

Sample assignment brief 1: Investigate different forms of communication

PROGRAMME NAME	BTEC Level 2 First Award in Health and Social Care
ASSIGNMENT TITLE	Investigate different forms of communication
ASSESSMENT EVIDENCE	Written report to include case studies and presentation notes

This assignment will assess the following learning aim and grading criteria:

Learning Aim A: Investigate different forms of communication

2A.P1 Describe different forms of verbal and non-verbal communication.

2A.P2 Describe different forms of alternative communication for different needs, using examples from health and social care.

2A.M1 Explain the advantages and disadvantages of different forms of communication used, with reference to a one-to-one and a group interaction.

2A.D1 Assess the effectiveness of different forms of communication for service users with different needs.

Scenario

You are volunteering at a local care centre. It could be a day centre or a residential centre for young people with disabilities or for older people with disabilities. As part of the induction process, you are asked to research a series of case studies that illustrate different forms of communication and then give a verbal presentation. Evidence presented verbally should be recorded. Detailed observation records/ witness testimonies should be completed and retained for internal and external verification.

• •

1. Give a detailed account of the forms of verbal communication skills, such as clear speech, appropriate language and age-appropriate language, pace, tone and pitch, non-discriminatory use of language and active listening skills. Non-verbal communication skills should include posture, facial expressions, eye contact, appropriate use of touch and personal space, gestures, non-threatening use of body language and personal space.

2. Describe the alternative forms of communication used for those who are visually impaired, hearing-impaired, or those with learning disabilities. Use examples of the different forms of communication you have used in a health and social care setting, or across different settings.

3. Explain the advantages and disadvantages of non-verbal, verbal and alternative forms of communication used in a one-to-one and a group interaction in health and social care.

4. (a) Assess the effectiveness of at least five different forms of communication, at least one of which must be an alternative form of communication.

    (b) Assess the effectiveness of these forms of communication for service users with needs such as visual or hearing impairments or learning difficulties.

Sample assignment brief 2: Investigate barriers to communication in health and social care

PROGRAMME NAME	BTEC Level 2 First Award in Health and Social Care
ASSIGNMENT TITLE	Investigate barriers to communication in health and social care
ASSESSMENT EVIDENCE	Written report to include case studies and presentation notes

This assignment will assess the following learning aim and grading criteria:

Learning Aim B: Investigate barriers to communication in health and social care

(2B.P3) Describe the barriers to communication in health and social care and their effects on service users.

(2B.P4) Using examples, explain ways in which barriers to communication may be overcome and the benefits to service users of overcoming these barriers

(2B.M2) Explain how measures have been implemented to overcome barriers to communication, with reference to a selected case.

(2B.D2) Evaluate the effectiveness of measures taken to remove barriers to communication, with reference to a selected case.

Scenario

You are volunteering at a local care centre. It could be a day centre or a residential centre for younger people with disabilities or for older people with disabilities. As part of the induction process, you are asked to investigate barriers to communication in health and social care, their effects and how to overcome the barriers.

Research and present a series of case studies then give a PowerPoint presentation. For the merit and distinction you may need to write notes to accompany your slides to cover the depth of analysis and the evaluation. Evidence presented verbally should be recorded. All notes should be retained for internal and external verification.

1. Describe the barriers to communication in health and social care and their effects on service users. Barriers could be environmental barriers, physical barriers, language barriers or due to social isolation. Describe the effects of barriers on individuals, such as not being able to have access to health and social care services, receiving poor quality health and social care, distress, increased social issues, and increased ill health.

   Remember to ensure confidentiality if using real case studies or you could use actual cases in the news.

2 (a) Use examples to explain how each type of barrier can be overcome by using the person's preferred method of communication and language, adjusting the physical environment and by effective non-verbal communication such as positive posture and facial expressions.

  (b) Explain the benefits to service users of overcoming these barriers.

3. Choose one of your case studies to develop in more depth and show how the measures you explained in 2 (a) have been put into practice to overcome barriers to communication.

4. Continue with the same example and say how successful the measures were in removing barriers. Say whether they were totally successful in removing barriers or partly successful, or were ineffective. Explain why you came to that decision.

Sample assignment brief 3: Communicate effectively in health and social care

PROGRAMME NAME	BTEC Level 2 First Award in Health and Social Care
ASSIGNMENT TITLE	Communicate effectively in health and social care
ASSESSMENT EVIDENCE	Completed observation checklist signed by an appropriate observer and learner reflective notes for each of the following situations: one-to-one communication, group communication

This assignment will assess the following learning aim and grading criteria:

Learning aim C: Communicate effectively in health and social care

2C.P5
Demonstrate communication skills through interactions in health and social care, describing their effects.

2C.M3
Select and demonstrate communication skills through interactions in health and social care, explaining their effectiveness.

2C.D3
Select and demonstrate communication skills through one-to-one and group interactions in health and social care, evaluating their effectiveness and making recommendations for improvement.

Scenario

You are volunteering at the day centre which Mr Norton attends. He has had a stroke and has difficulty speaking. He is also weak down one side and needs help to walk with his walking frame. He has poor eyesight. Take the role of a care worker and discuss Mr Norton's care with him to check that he is satisfied with the care and whether any changes need to be made. You will be observed and assessed on this. Later, in a group situation you will need to present your findings and discuss this with the rest of the team. If this is carried out in a simulated role-play situation, video recording may be helpful.

Task

1. Select and demonstrate appropriate communication skills in both a one-to-one and a group situation describing their effects. An observer checklist should accompany your own reflective account for each situation. Communication skills include active listening, body language, facial expression, eye contact, the use of appropriate language, tone of voice, and pace of speech, proximity, clarifying and repeating.

2. Use your notes to reflect on the skills you selected and applied and the appropriateness of the communication methods you used for different service users. Say how effective you think your communication skills were in the interaction.

3 (a) Develop your explanation of your own effectiveness and come to a conclusion about it in the one-to-one and group situation.

   (b) Based on this, make recommendations for how you could improve your communication skills in each situation.

Assessment criteria

Level 2 Pass	Level 2 Merit	Level 2 Distinction
Learning aim A: Investigate different forms of communication		
2A.P1 Describe different forms of verbal and non-verbal communication.	**2A.M1** Explain the advantages and disadvantages of different forms of communication used, with reference to a one-to-one and a group interaction.	**2A.D1** Assess the effectiveness of different forms of communication for service users with different needs.
2A.P2 Describe different forms of alternative communication for different needs, using examples from health and social care.		
Learning aim B: Investigate barriers to communication in health and social care		
2B.P3 Describe the barriers to communication in health and social care and their effects on service users.	**2B.M2** Explain how measures have been implemented to overcome barriers to communication, with reference to a selected case.	**2B.D2** Evaluate the effectiveness of measures taken to remove barriers to communication, with reference to a selected case.
2B.P4 Using examples, explain ways in which barriers to communication may be overcome and the benefits to service users of overcoming these barriers.		
Learning aim C: Communicate effectively in health and social care		
2C.P5 Demonstrate communication skills through interactions in health and social care, describing their effects.	**2C.M3** Select and demonstrate communication skills through interactions in health and social care, explaining their effectiveness.	**2C.D3** Select and demonstrate communication skills through one-to-one and group interactions in health and social care, evaluating their effectiveness and making recommendations for improvement.

Knowledge recap answers

Learning aim A

1. Sender – the person starting the communication; Message – what the sender wishes to communicate; Medium – the method of communication, whether verbal, written, signed, electronic or telephone; Receiver – the person who receives the message and interprets it; Understanding – the message has to be correctly interpreted by the receiver; and Feedback – the receiver needs to show the sender that he or she has received and understood the message.
2. Verbal and non-verbal communication.
3. Visual impairment, hearing impairment, learning disabilities and/or brain injury following accident or disease.
4. Makaton.

Learning aim B

1. Environmental, physical, language, social isolation.
2. Reduced access to health and social care services, poor quality of delivery of health and social care, distress, increased social issues, increased ill health.
3. Preferred method of communication, preferred language, adaptations to the physical environment, effective non-verbal communication.
4. Increased access to health and social care, improved quality of health and social care delivery, reduction of emotional distress, increased involvement in interactions, raised levels of self-esteem, reduced frustration.

Learning aim C

1. Active listening, body language, facial expression, eye contact if appropriate, use of appropriate language, tone of voice, pace of speech, proximity, clarifying, repeating.
2. What happened? What worked? What did not work? What would I change to improve it next time?
3. Selecting a method that works for both the sender and the receiver of the message. For example, a visual method such as facial expression can aid effective communication when people have hearing problems.
4. If we only make recommendations, nothing changes or improves. It is only when we carry out those recommendations that we get improvement.

THE LIBRARY
TOWER HAMLETS COLLEGE
POPLAR HIGH STREET
LONDON E14 0AF
Tel: 0207 510 7763

Index

Index